This book is for the promotion of a safe and healthy growth for the generations to come. keep calm and remain strong. Like a bird sing your song, play your role as we time travel along.

Luis Daniel Rosado Sr.

Book Of I

Our knowledge expands like the radius of the foundation to a towering mound of sand collecting over time.

Remain aware of where you end up in time, for your fate can change like the flip of a dime.

**A Drop of blood, down the river of Time.
1**

Chapter 1, Boy to Man ...

There once lived a man who sheltered alone. Inside a building made of brick and stone. The man was once a boy just like you. Learn from the great things he went through. From the moonlight in the night to the sunlight in the day, for I am your father and will brighten the way. In a single room for long periods of time, the sound of isolation helped the soul start to unwind. Then a magical question had come to mind. I ask myself "Who am I?", I am who I am, that of a man partner to a woman that keeps us human. Instantly other great questions came to thy mind. "Where did I come from, where am I going and why am I here?"LDRS Questions we don't ask daily hidden in our orbital sphere. There once stood a weak man who spoke them clear. I asked thy Father but heard no sound. For life is a journey and we are space bound.

Left from right and right from wrong, will keep us strong as we time travel along. One second at a time is a good pace, don't forget your place. We are not in a race, just traveling through space. At your own pace, you shall embrace. From that moment forward I slowed my pace, made some plans to begin developing my space. Place a level corner stone at your base for a strong foundation on the way to space. A corner stone to a good foundation is to keep your eye open to exploration. Over time opportunity will glow, like a bright light forming from a shadow. Follow the energy so you know where to go, just watch for where it ends its flow. Take your time and plan life slow, learn from your history so you know where not to go. Never chase what may appear, too good to have I will make it clear.

Thy throne is where you rest thy head, feel safe with thy family when you break thy bread. Gain knowledge in thy youth, thus learn the truth.

Chapter 2 Why in the Road?

Rivers and roads travel side by side, like climbing a latter and going down the slide. Rather the river or road is splitting or merging the facts are clear, know your way and have no fear. If you ever feel lost just remember the sun sets in the west, so you can rest. The sun is highest in the southern sky every noon unless you travel south of the moon. When you rest your head be sure to stay rooted, for when you arise your system is rebooted. Muladhara is thy grounding energy, keep it grounded and experience life's synergy. Four red roses ready to sprout, out thy crown chakra the energy will spout.

Nights to days flow so right don't fight your sleep just have a great flight. Through faith or science Adam or Atom will guide the way, careful on these journeys where most are left astray. For day by day time will pass, your family tree will grow like grass. With roots so deep in mother earth, your father planted the seed that lead to your birth. A time and place marked in space with a x&y, for two bloodlines have merged you will learn why. Learning from the great and tragic facts of your early bloodline, will guide you to the great triumphs that begin to shine. Systems are created and destroyed, beware of where you become employed. For thy soul is not for sale, don't become another tail. For when the head begins to fail, it is time for you to bail. Mind your own business and stay on track, for all true followers will have your back. A knife in the rear is like a spear, collect them up for karma will have thy enemies quivering in fear.

Shed no tears when souls come and go, on and off stage just like a show. Take control and play your roll, like a walk in the park it will be a stroll.

Chapter 3 ABCD 1234 ...

Matrix of cubes stacked up nice and neat, like waves of a sound that skip no beat. For 1-9 are absolute, we count forever and keep time like the beat of a flute. A-Z are reserved for symbols of sounds, while both share patterns in leaps and bounds. Emotion can be expressed in sound, "oh Yes!" how profound. Music is found all around; even birds that may look free are matrix bound. Other symbols make up other languages and sounds, with shapes that may look out of bounds. With puzzles and hidden knowledge all around, one day you will be ready to go space bound. From an earth platform with leaps and bounds, you can stand in space where there are no grounds. Rooting thy soul will keep you from losing your place, whether traveling on earth or up in space.

The human race has lost its place. With no foundation they lost their base. Having no direction who is to say, what is real and what is a play. Knowing when to make a correction, while leaving the masses in suspension. Like aimless sheep searching for direction, for I am your father and this book is protection.

Chapter 4, Grounded ...

Stay grounded my children for life is a mystery, while thy past remains history. Mythical story or not, life is still a trip, stay light not dark and please don't flip. Being grounded starts while you are alone, meditating inside your temple upon you're thrown. Focus on Rosetta Stone, for when thy mind is open your reality will be blown. Pay close attention to what you're shown, for one day it will be your own. Language is simple just making sound; it will expand your knowledge to what is all around. Keep in mind what you have found, tell no soul for they will have you bound.

Red color light emanating from your root, like a shock of energy from there will shoot. Up to the next chakra it will flow, that energy center will make you feel mellow. For its color is yellow, like sun flowers in a meadow. Soon you will learn of that center's powers, while studying its magic for hours. During the spring showers, in a field full of flowers. Building a strong foundation to hold large towers but not in the physical and spending no dollars. From the root to the crown, keep a smile not a frown. Colors outside black or brown, keep your head up and not down. Enjoy thy life and never stop to travel. Steer clear of those who hold a gavel, for they spread false judgments and will soon be made gravel. Muladhara is the name, for this energy is to blame. Dark red like a phoenix flame, reborn from its ashes while evolving threw the game. My sons have no shame, when you fail if you learn you will not be the same. When you study your chakras you will see, everything you need is inside you or me. So learn to create what you want in this reality.

I
Before
Thyself
2

Chapter 1, Traveling up the Creek.

As the bloodlines travel down the river of time and away from their source, I began to backstroke up the river with no remorse. Learn thy history and get it right, even if you're up all night. Fight for what you believe is right, keep it in sight for you will always be guided by the light. Looking back at a shadow so dark, history is like a bomb and you are the spark. Culture, Religion, Politics, and Class will keep you guessing about the glass. Is it half full or empty, does not matter for having some is plenty. Never take more than your fair share, unless you're asked to indulge now that is rare.

Be aware of what you drink and eat, for some hands can be dirtier than feet. It can make you sicker then spoiled meat. Traveling from land to land just understand, you should only eat when you can't resist the delicious smells at hand. For fowl beasts where made to roam just don't cook or kill them in your home. We have plenty of food planted upon mother earth, as a daily gift she bares food like birth. Spoil none for she likes to consume, of what she offers so return her some soon. Fruits and vegetables make a great diet, better if you grow them so you don't have to buy it. Herbs, spices, nuts and honey are great to share, even if your neighbor is a greedy bear. Beware of others who play a good role, just remember a good friend could fall off like a mole. As you travel your bloodline you will learn, nothing is free so give and you shall earn.

Chapter 2 A walk in the park.

As time travels bloodlines dry up, for death comes for all so never give up. Keep your head held high, never tell a lie, even if it will make others cry, don't be shy. The truth hurts but will keep you free, just be ready for when it is time to flee. The truth can cost you your life my son, the less you say the more you have won. Keep your love ones close but your enemies closer, they will all destroy your heart just like a bull dozer. Trust is hard to gain, give out to much and it will cause heavy pain. Time heals all from season to season, like a walk in the park the different views change with deep reason. Putting others first is a good practice. Although some will leave you as dry as a cactus. Love your family and remain strong, even if you feel they are just dragging you along, like the cycle of a repetitive song.

Chapter 3 Gone with the wind.

Once or twice in a lifetime there will come many, with nothing to offer you shall still give plenty. While traveling abroad you shall see that karma brings all you need. For while you are at home you plant the seed to learn how to distance you from greed. Your bloodline will guide thy way, stand fast my son don't go astray. Save time to play for after you pray, bow thy head and say. "Thank you Father for this blessed day, to you my time I pay." For love and lust is a dangerous game, where no one wins but we are all to blame. You will surely learn its twists and turns, just pray it never itch or burns. Lust is what you want and yearn, but to find true love you must wait your turn. Time will pass and if you wait, then surely you will have a full plate.

Sacral energy deep down in your second dwelling, creative energy will keep you spelling. Keep it clean or it will start smelling, love shall always be free so don't get caught buying or selling. Don't buy what is free at home, even if you're at a beach in Rome. If you are married and abandoned alone, just meditated inside your temple upon thy throne. Avoid the urge to play alone, even when it is hard as a bone. Living in a glass house we throw no stone, as they run from your face but act hard on the phone. Family of clowns funny bones, broken pockets money loans. They will steal your time like money cones, leaving your accounts frozen like ice cream cones. Sting them like a bee while building your honey comb, have them crashing back to earth when they hit the astrodome. Space bound is a dream never shown, like a hot air balloon it was blown.

Chapter 4, Sex or Sexy.

Sex is a subject many will frown, for here is where they are let down. The magic of creation is not for play, some will think they have to discharge every day. Listen my sons for I shall say, leave it alone and go to pray. Negative energy here will lead you astray, keep your phallus clean or you shall pay. Wait for when you are wedded and ready, that time will come so keep your mind steady. Remember love and lust has its twists and turns, so your partner must be one who lives and learns. Open minds are awake, while a small mind is squared and baked like a cake. Too many layers to break through like an onion you will get sick too. Teaching one who will not learn, don't waste your time just wait your turn. All has reason, just wait your season. Time is all you have so wait, just never tell yourself it is too late.

When you rush things they fall apart, keep a focus mind just like a dart. Keep thy mind sharp like the pit of a peach, while keeping it open like the mass of a beach. Learn and refine as you teach, just remain aware when you begin to preach. There are those who will try and reverse your speech and those who will get stuck like a leach. Sucking your soul they drain you like batteries, then try and keep you around with their stories and flatteries. This is when you use your masteries, to get insight on their mysteries. For small minds repeat from others, while an awaken mind will know thy brothers. Respect all women as if they were your mother. Avoid trinkets and save on clutter. Travel through life like a knife in butter. Be aware of storms and close your shutter. A woman flaunting her body has no brains, so she uses it for gains. Your wife will respect her vessel as one with her body, and vowed to not share it with **anybody**.

*Here
Now
and
Forever
3*

Chapter 1, Where Am I.

Coming up on a 10 year milestone meditating on my mental throne. I don't know if I should moan or groan. This life is like grass, it is overgrown. Living in a glass house, how dare they throw a stone? Scars in my back like thick skin, it is never shown. I will never wish this knowledge to become unknown.
I rented a studio then purchased a home. Using all the knowledge I gathered up inside my dome. All the seeds that I have sown, forsaken am I for little has grown.

For nights in the ocean to the days at sea, my soul still urges to just flee. Locked up by the winter's cold, we wait for the spring glee to unfold. The flowers, colors, birds and that bee, all these changes happen every year you shall see. We are not all as free as you and me. So plan your future and you shall see. We spring into the summer for 2 months and watch time spin, for fall ushers in the cold of winter to lock us up again. Land mass rising out of the sea, oceans separate you and me. Like a horizon upon an open sea, how do we know where are we? Traveling from here to there, where are we going and when do we get there? The sun will always rise in the east, be sure to pray before morning feast. Do not consume any beast for you will gain the least.

The same goes for lunch when the sun is up high, a small meal can hold you by. The sun will set to the west, pray before dinner then lay your vessel to rest. As your spirit lay in its nest, you just dream of what is best. Just know thy son for you are blessed, just pray to your father when you are stressed. I placed my love both near and far, hair in the wind and a silent guitar. How have I made it thus far?, I am proud to say I stayed out of the bar. Mom said dad had a problem well so do I, so I lay down and I cry. Am I weak? Oh no not I. At least I try. Will I die if I lie? For am I perfect oh no not I. Cry when you lie for guilt travels by, even the truth will have you asking why. Feeling the pain of false punishment comes often, just close your eyes and in any language count to ten.

Common sense died in my age, which is why this world is full of rage. Careful when you turn the page, a simple cut will have you feeling strange.

Chapter 2 Butterflies in the Belly.
Emotion passed by one day, mother said finish dinner before I can play. I ate my food all in one bite, now my belly is not feeling right. Unlike a pain sometimes it feels funny, now we have a butterfly in our tummy. Emotions weak or strong at times, like sweet fruit or limes. A strong light bright like yellow, meditate right or you will be feeling mellow. Unlike a sturdy bowl of fruit you will be feeling jello. You shall find what you are seeking, just close your eyes and remember no peaking. When the energy is flowing right, you will sleep all through the night. Fall asleep without a fight, awaken ready to take flight.

Manipura flies in the third sphere remain aware what happens here. Break a smile or shed a tear, just never hide from a fear. Energy rise as it comes near, just wait to celebrate until it is clear. Don't always follow what you hear, even if it is followed by a cheer. Butterflies evolving from here to there, judge yourself for you know what is fair. Never grab her by the hair, unless you're fighting with a bear. Life will keep you running around, from corner to corner matrix bound. What you see will be profound, keep it all a secret make no sound. They won't believe you oh no they won't. I have tried and I tried and still they don't. The truth from prophets gets us killed, while negative profits just get billed. Slaves play with money while lost in time so I try to help when, when I bust a rhyme. Keep it humble commit no crime. Plan your future waste no time.

Chapter 3, Trust.

Trust no soul for you shall see, that lies and deception sting like a bee. Trust no bank for they steal in the name of a fee, just save or invest your money and remember nothing is free. Trust is hard to earn, take your time and you shall learn. This world is built by human slavery, careful who you speak to most careless about bravery. Liars hate the truth, learn as much as you can in your youth. Be sure to play an instrument or sports, create an archive and save all your reports. Truth is backed by facts, that is what opinion lacks. Broken road full of cracks, sheeple lying on their backs. Trust only your blood brother he will trust you back, respect him back and raise each other like a jack. Carry each other like a pack, over the shoulder or on your back. Unconditional love you shall not lack.

Chapter 4, Chakra.

The chakras are points of energy in the body where the soul can translate information. Like energy flowing from dimension to dimension in any direction. Each having its own theme to follow, study well or you shall remain hollow. Like a vessel with no crew, lost in the ocean blue. Remain aware of reality, like its invisible factors such as gravity. The masses will have you guessing about your mentality while little do they understand their own immortality. Build your eagle for it will soar, if you bare children teach them more. Appreciate the next generation so we can evolve, as the close minded classes continue to dissolve. Seven chakras from root to crown, red to white but no black or brown. Mind, body and soul work as one, learn more now and you have won. Morals light up the way, stay focused so you don't go astray.

Together
we are
Lost in
Time
4

Chapter 1, *All value equals Time...*

Memories from when I was two years old, a black horse my father and grandfather had to hold. Nice and tight so it won't flee, they walk on each side of me. Twenty seven years in the past, I can't believe time can go by so fast. I miss them oh very so, I know they travel beside my soul. Now they watch over us yes you and bro, one day I will join them and you will know. The soul inside is timeless you shall see, the physical body shall pass like a bee. From season to season we come and go, lose your memory until you learn what I know. Leaving clues behind and stories to share, this information will prove to be rare.

Thus beautiful to the masses or appealing to the ear, just know most of your fellow friends will stay lost in the rear. Life will change but you shall gain plenty, just never leave your brother with his mind empty. Spaces fill with both good and bad, too much of one will leave you both sad. Time is a tool you shall hold deer, or else you risk being lost in the rear. Never bring thy brother pain, unconditional love is the best to gain. Even while traveling in the pouring rain, brothers walk hand and hand while they share their pain. I love you both equally oh yes I do, just remember everything I teach you. Help your mother with all at hand, for you are the singer and she is your band. Listen closely to the tones of life as we travel along, not missing a beat will keep the family strong. Use your voice loud and clear, keeping what you say sharp as a spear.

Chapter 2 One beat per second.

Never take time for granted, it is the most important as I have ranted. One second to make a choice, careful it can leave you with no voice. Surely in your mind where you are free, for in the matrix you will pay a fee. Freedom of speech is no longer free, I watched it die right in front of me. Technology has a hold on us, be aware of what you say on the bus. Repeating a lie will never make it true, unlike the truth a lie will travel like the flu. From near and far they will watch and rage, since the beginning of time to the end of the page. Religions pass through time just like a phase, churches, temples and mosks all go up in a blaze. Conquer them all one at a time as if you're traveling thru a maze. Never stop moving or stay stuck in a daze.

Sadness all around us like a blaze, darkness overtakes us like a royal flush of spades. Light comes in many rays and in different shades, it can brighten your way or leave you on ice skating blades.

Chapter 3, *A night in the wind.*

A brisk summer night long ago, under the stars to sleep I go. Rest my eyes to the chillful breeze, said a prayer while I asked father please. Guard thy vessel through the night awaken to the sun so bright. Never thought I would reach this height but all I have done is stand and fight. When your own blood stabs you in the back, just stay in the light and like a shadow they will be consumed by the black. Never spill the sands of time, nor waste thy energy on a crime. Let them talk and choke on lies, while you sit back and hear their cries.

Sirens cry out so very loud, don't fall asleep just stand up proud. Time square is a beating heart, though polluted like a dirty fart. From a distance she is beautiful like a piece of art, she is also full of the Quickie Mart. Hit Wall Street's bulls eye with a speeding dart, runaway money train about to depart. Hearts full of gold have a blackout; blood fills the streets like an endless waterspout. One hundred ways in but no way out, surrounded by water but still in a drought. Lose your way better find a rought, get lost and stay while you cry and pout. You will never know what this is all about, until you close your eyes and let your spirit out. A loving heart and a kind soul, a good man left behind so dull. Careful what you learn to roll, it will keep you at the bottom of the totem pole. Open your heart for all around to see, from mountain top to shining sea.

Be ready for the time to flee, remember those who guided you like me.

Chapter 4, Names...

{God} can be greats or demonics, for names and titles are just harmonics. Awake or asleep you shall be, a sheeple or shepherd we shall see. For when it is time to flee, you will obey your four fathers the ones before me. Hollow be thy name, so many names but they are all the same. Noah spoke it upon his birth; let me show you what it is worth. JHWH with no vowel is the name, never put it to shame. Like a deep sneeze or exhale, you will hear god bless you without fail. Book of Enoch is a great read, seventh from Adam yes he who planted the first seed. For Noah was the 10th generation, after the flood the world was open to exploration. Noah his three sons and their wives survived the devastation, along with many animals they were ready for rejuvenation.

Noah spoke but the truth fell upon deaf ears. Jesus, Moses, Muhammad and more shed tears. Still to this day the truth is hidden to plain fear. Fear of death or isolation, have no fear just use meditation. Stay true my son the way is clear; just be careful for what you hear. Learn from all your mistakes in life, don't just live to please your wife. The more you give the less they love, for materialism doesn't come from above. Worldly trinkets are for small minds, save and travel for great finds. Explore the world for its glory, document all and share your story. History is his-story so, never let anyone tell you no. Let them act as you run the show. Like running water time will flow.

In The
Shadow
there is
Light
5

Chapter 1, The Darkness that follows...

Tears for a history so long and dark, meditating for days without a spark. Free in the ocean call me a shark, keep your vessel moving forward never stay in park. From a slave at home to a slave of Rome, we still belong to the English throne. Spain conquered us like human trade; at least that is what our history portrayed. Lies upon lies just another theory, even the truth will keep you weary. From one man we come and go, year upon year they made us into a show. We shine so bright our energies flow, like piss in the wind just hope it don't blow. Mother's the slave while father's the owner, obelisk the symbol yes an erect boner.

Born into debt now who are the owners, this country is full of moaners and groaners. Believing they are truly free, I can't wait to just flee. A burning pain inside of me, I still don't know just who are we. From where do we came to where we are, all I know we have traveled very far. Have no limits just set the bar, even if we can't reach the closest star. Lost in space maybe a joke, like a finger in your eye just do not poke. For freedom of speech hangs at the end of a rope, I don't know how long we can cope. Dirty handouts with no soup, I pray my son you lost no hope. Many men's hearts fail them so their found hanging from a rope, careful depression is a dangerous slope. Lack of love from your mate, leave your mind going irate. Respect them all as if they were your mother, unconditional love as if they were thy brother. Physical love is strong so respect it, once it is gone it is gone just forget it.

Chapter 2 Giving to empty hands.

Giving is great just careful the gift, too much materials will leave you a drift. Love cannot be purchased its true, once you stop giving they stop loving you. Lies and rumors fill the air, like the smell of dung at the county fair. The more you give the less you are appreciated, for once you stop giving you become hated. Never ask for what you don't need, for a spear in the back just to watch it bleed. Even if your planting a positive seed, only ask if you desperately need. Never sell your love my son, not even for a night of fun. It will keep you on the run, you're better off hanging with a nun. For all we have is time I say, so use it right or you will pay. Don't forget to laugh and play, just as you learned to stop and pray. Holidays will come and go, no point in spending time or money for most are just for show. Nothing holy about them, just spit them out as you do a flem. Just days to confuse the truth my son, while they spend their savings on things they call fun. You don't have to run and hide, just show respect and know the truth inside.

Chapter 3, Spells.

When using shapes called characters that later turn into sounds, you can create actions it is so profound. Creating a spell can bring others a smell or a ring in the ear even have them trembling in fear. Shed no tear for those stuck in a spell, for their weakness they shall remain in hell. A dark place where all goes wrong, not the fiery place of where you hear in song. For hell is a mindset and so is heaven, just like comparing six to seven. For thy soul returns every four to five generations so learn your four fathers and keep the rotations. Be sure to build thy families wealth, keep it safe yes very stealth.

Vishuddha is the name of this place where spells come to life when you speak into space. Say thy grace but not in the verbal, for your conversations are not with a turtle. Create your world inside your mind then with your words let it unwind. Create your spells then maintain thy words, for you will be souring among the birds. Make plans then spell them out, have faith and kill all doubt. For negativity can be found all about so stay aware when you shout. Like a wave or water spout what you say can keep you out. From group to group know what to say, as they compete you can play. All sides can't win but you can gain, as long as you just us your brain. Keep your opinion to thyself as you play all sides just like an elf. Always give to those in need, be aware of those full of greed. For thy goods will be lost with speed, then you will be left with no seed. Plant them far so they don't spoil, careful to not invest in oil.

For monopolies are hard to break, take one cow make many steak. Spoiled meat mixed with fake who knows what we eat, just eat what you grow and make. Easy on the sweets and cake, cooking is fun but even more fun to bake. Grow your fish in your lake, ocean fish are sick for father sake. One third of the waters is his to take, just check the bible this is not fake.

Chapter 4, Communication

Know more then what you say, for when you speak just know your way. Always take some time to pray and you shall never be lead astray. Play as a dog and know when to stay, your mind is a muscle exercise it every day. Your voice is Strong so use it wise, just be sure to tell no lies. Attend to those who start to cry, especially when someone dies. Don't get labeled as a spy even if it is a lie. Shoot down you eagle they will try so even higher you shall fly. Away from the dark and into the light for your future will be so bright. No need to fight if you are right. For the facts shall hold their might. Big mouth but little bite, keep all they enemies close yes in plain sight. Every move you shall know for your living in their shadow. Never take what is not yours and you will be granted behind the next doors. Stay grounded upon the floors, be aware of the mores. Begging till there is nothing left, leave them all and stay blest. They will jump on their own, just like a dog after its bone. Empty minds have no throne, just an empty temple and no one is home. Trojan horse is still parked inside of Rome, Holy Sea capped by a golden dome. Russia has one of these pawns to; they will spend their life trying to crucify you. Choose no side for they are all to lose, just ask Noah who is the one to choose. Israelite is my skin; it is also what I am within. Not a group or Nation we are not white or Caucasian. Rare bread upon this land, we give to the many but they have eaten our hand. I shall never understand.

Hidden
Book
of
1
6

Chapter 1 A Time long ago

The days ran long without a worry in sight, our futures seemed so bright. Guided slightly by the light, we never had to fight. Living life as a youth, now working hard inside a booth. Told the future but it was not regarded as the truth. Time passed and the light began to fade, tedious times arrived like walking on a blade. Times that come darker then a spade no light like sitting in the shade. Ill decisions that I made, even more the light began to fade. Living life in the shadow of fear, I learned to leave history in the rear.

Unable to teach what is not know, my knowledge arrived after I was grown. Like a hot air balloon my mind was blown. Filled with intelligence from a higher source, I learned what I could with no remorse. Learning to ride and falling off my high horse, being kicked while I was down but not losing my course. The evil lies around my temple, kept me inside and living so simple. Smile big and flash your dimples, in your teen years don't pop your pimples. They will spread like lies in the wind, make you feel as if you have sinned. Others will put you down show no frown for you are wearing the crown. Your enemies will look like clowns, ugly and evil laughing through their broken frowns. We all have our ups and downs, they will come just Like numbered rounds.

Chapter 2 Wo-man

Beautiful songs from the sirens crashed many vessels while leaving many men without vests upon their souls. Heed the sirens as a warning of danger for love can leave you stuck with a stranger. Control your lust, my sons you must think twice before you trust. Save your love for the right woman that will treat you as an equal human. Mistakes can't be taken back so learn from me, follow your heart and leave the rest be. For you will see the pain is worse than being stung by a bee. Careful where you plant your tree, be sure it is after you take a knee. Wedded by thy Father is free, it don't count if you have to pay a fee. Special day my son you will see.

Chapter 3 Thy Temple.

Not in the physical no not by far, for thy temple is like a shooting star. A place so bright it can light up the night. If seen from space it would be a great sight. Thy temple is truly a holy place, ear, eyes, nose and mouth so you can manipulate space. Learn to listen before you speak, just hold your tongue inside your beak. For information is all we seek, the wrong words can have you floating down the creek. Always kiss your mother on the cheek, close your eyes as you pray and do not peek. Intuition is information from within, gather it up and you shall win. Common sense is no longer common, unless it is from a guru or an old shaman. The truth will be hard to find, but I found it and I am blind. They say the blind will lead the sighted, so when I speak they get excited.

Silence can prove good at times, but natural sounds will have you talking rhymes. Knowledge will have you seeing signs, shining so bright just don't close the blinds. A dark vial covers their eyes, easier for them to accept the lies. Even after one hundred tries, they will just annoy you like a pack of flies. Keep thy temple clean from all hate, never get stuck in an unfair debate. The mass of aimless sheep, just sit back and off the cliff they shall leap. For every sheppard they have killed, and with a wolf the spot was filled. Brands flow on all the cattle, funny how they think they are the ones in the saddle. Little do they know they have lost the battle, they are easy to control with the swipe of a gavel.

Fear no man for your fathers stand ready; have your enemies quivering like a bowl of spaghetti.

Chapter 4, MISSING.

Puzzle pieces all around, collect them all as I have found. Multiple puzzles stacked nice and neat, I still have to build just like a beat. Slow and steady it will take time, absorb it all just like slime. Another book is to come with vast information leave no crumb. Indulge in the light where it will not burn, just sit back and wait your turn. The crown is still on the way, as you wait you can go out and play. For when some time has passed you by and in thy vessel you learn to fly. All your limits surely will die, freedom is waiting but not in the sky. The physical realm is just one piece of the pie, if they tell you otherwise it is just a lie. The facts are clear I have done my job, I give plenty but still get called a snob.

Feast with the many just don't become a slob. Wash your hand and use the towel to open the door knob. If you fall get right back up, refill your cup and never give up. Have no shame this is all part of the game, on your way to fame if you fail only you are to blame. Give this book another read, try it at a slower speed, if you need to plant a seed keep in mind it is another mouth to feed. Never fill thy mind with greed, for all you have is all you need. Give my sons I will plead all my knowledge you shall heed. I love you with a full heart sorry if we are to part.

The Future Brings Great Gifts for those who Wait

.....

Made in the USA
Columbia, SC
25 February 2020